STARTING OUT

BICYCLES

I0895847

LORI DITTMER

CREATIVE EDUCATION • CREATIVE PAPERBACKS

CONT

ENTS

I AM A BICYCLE.

I ride on streets and paths.

Look at my two wheels and my handlebars!

A rider sits in the saddle and steers with my handlebars.

We go to school or work. Sometimes, we ride just for fun.

The rider pushes the pedals.

The chain moves and makes the tires roll.

I can go 15 miles (24.1 km) per hour. Whee!!

My bell rings to let others know that I am near.

When it's time to stop, the rider squeezes the brake. Then my kickstand swings down.

I am ready for the next ride!

MAKE A NOISE

wHIR

RRRR!

Can you make a bicycle noise? They click, squeak, whoosh, and rattle.

Listen to these sounds:

Now it is your turn!

BICYCLE WORDS

Handlebars: Where a bike rider puts their hands to make the bike go in the right direction

Kickstand: A metal rod attached to the bottom of a bicycle that holds it up

Saddle: The seat on a bicycle

READING CORNER

Arnold, Quinn. *Bicycles*. Mankato, Minn.: Creative Education and Creative Paperbacks, 2020.

Black, Nessa. *Biking*. North Mankato, Minn.: Amicus, 2020.

Toolen, Avery. *From Metal to Bicycle*. Minneapolis: Bullfrog Books, 2022.

INDEX

PUBLISHED BY CREATIVE EDUCATION AND CREATIVE PAPERBACKS
P.O. Box 227, Mankato, Minnesota 56002
Creative Education and Creative Paperbacks are imprints of The Creative Company
www.thecreativecompany.us

COPYRIGHT © 2026 CREATIVE EDUCATION, CREATIVE PAPERBACKS
International copyright reserved in all countries. No part of this book may be reproduced in any form without written permission from the publisher.

LIBRARY OF CONGRESS CATALOGING-IN-PUBLICATION DATA
Names: Dittmer, Lori author
Title: Bicycles / Lori Dittmer.
Description: Mankato, Minnesota : Creative Education and Creative Paperbacks, [2026] | Series: Starting out | Includes bibliographical eferences and index. | Audience: Ages 4-7 | Audience: Grades K-1 | Summary: "Introduce beginning readers to a day on the sidewalk with a bicycle in this STEM starter. Includes photos, a labeled vehicle diagram, "Make a Noise" section, glossary, and further resources"— Provided by publisher.
Identifiers: LCCN 2025013144 (print) | LCCN 2025013145 (ebook) | ISBN 9798895810255 library binding | ISBN 9781682779781 paperback | ISBN 9798895811511 ebook
Subjects: LCSH: Bicycles"—Juvenile literature | CYAC: Bicycles and bicycling
Classification: LCC TL412 .D58 2026 (print) | LCC TL412 (ebook) | DDC 629.227/2"— dc23/eng/20250604
LC record available at https://lccn.loc.gov/2025013144
LC ebook record available at https://lccn.loc.gov/2025013145

DESIGN AND PRODUCTION
Design by Rhea Magaro
Art direction by Graham Morgan

PHOTOGRAPHS BY
Dreamstime/Eugene Onischenko, 2, Fuzja44, 6, Ljupco, 12; Getty Images/C Squared Studios, 4, carlosalvarez, 14, George Doyle, 5, IlexImage, 11, Westend61, 10; Pexels/Markus Spiske, 8; Shutterstock/arturnichiporenko, cover; Unsplash/Chris Henry, 7; Wikimedia Commons/Granada, 9

Every effort has been made to contact copyright holders for material reproduced in this book. Any omissions will be rectified in subsequent printings if notice is given to the publisher.

Printed in the United States